COME OUT ALIVE

Essential Survival Strategies and Information to Keep You and Your Family Safe During Natural Disasters, War, Civil Unrest, and Terror Attacks

2

Table of Contents

Introduction

The news is full of upsetting incidents from category four hurricanes to potential missile launches from North Korea. Now is the time to ensure you have everything in place to keep you and your family safe no matter where you live.

Natural disasters, war, civil unrest and terror attacks can happen anywhere, at any time, and you must have some essential survival strategies in place to maintain your safety.

Surviving any bad situation is about preparedness. If you lack preparation, then you will feel panic, fear and are less likely to survive than someone who has thought about what they would do in various situations.

Throughout the information provided, you will find some specific preparedness details for certain disasters to help you prepare for these problems versus an overall survival guide.

You are still going to have some steps to follow and use in any emergency situation that may arise; however, natural disasters, war, civil unrest and terror attacks will also have a chapter.

Everyone wants to survive, and you can ensure you and your family is safe when you train for the most likely events to plague you, as well as prepare for emergency needs.

Discover how you can make your family safe in times of heightened turmoil.

Chapter 1: Essential Steps, Training, and Equipment

Each situation will require different training and reactions. However, if you have the basics down, you are more likely to survive than someone who has never considered emergency situations.

Essential Steps

Begin by listing the types of situations you may find yourself facing. It is best to think about what may happen in the area where you are currently living. For example, a mountainous region known for floods is a place where you would need snow, rain and fire survival skills. The floods occur when it rains continuously for several days, and the rivers and lakes become too full of water. Fires can start due to lightning and thunderstorms, while blizzards can occur in the winter months rendering a person stranded in their vehicle.

If you live in the Middle East, Europe or major cities around the world, terror attacks, war and civil unrest are more likely.

1. Start by outlining the potential emergency issues that may arise in your local area.

2. Find training for situations you may find yourself in, whether it is surviving a blizzard without power or in a vehicle, triaging in an area of civil unrest, etc.

3. Update or take CPR/First Aid courses.

4. Prepare a "go" bag.

5. Make it easy to grab all your important documents in the event of an emergency.

6. Listen to the news; especially, the weather and information about war, civil unrest, and terror attacks. Being informed ensures you are ready if something occurs in your area.

7. Follow the guidelines given by local officials. For example, in a hurricane zone, if authorities tell you to leave—go—do not hesitate.

8. Have an evacuation plan, and know the different paths you can take out of the area in the event one route is blocked, you can immediately go another way.

9. Drive the various escape routes from your area to become comfortable with them.

10. Have an emergency kit, fire extinguisher, and road kit in every vehicle you own.

The above ten steps will save you in any emergency you may become involved in when a disaster occurs.

Training

There are two types of training: survival and first aid/CPR. YMCAs, libraries, clinics and the Red Cross are just a few places that offer yearly first aid/CPR courses. If you have never taken a course before—do so immediately. For those who have not had a course in the last five years—enroll. CPR and first aid rules have changed in the last few years, and it is imperative that you re-certify.

Survival training can take on many forms. Typically, courses are set up based on the natural disasters or circumstances that may affect your area. Do not think you are safe from a terror attack simply because you live away from war-torn countries, civil unrest or a major city. Anything can happen. You may be flying for a vacation and find yourself a part of a devious plot where survival skills become necessary.

Colleges, universities, YMCAs, libraries, the Red Cross and other organizations offer survival training. For example, mountain shops in Colorado provide survival training for blizzards, floods, hiking and climbing accidents.

Courses teach you how to assess, become calm and react to the most serious issue in the situation first, before tackling the minor problems. Everyone will respond to emergencies differently. But, the more you think about it, analyze, and consider facing problems that may arise, the easier it is for your brain to adapt when something does occur.

For example, what would you do if a bear broke into your home? In survival training, you are told not to run, not to make sudden movements, and to make yourself appear bigger than you are by making a lot of noise. But, could you react in that manner?

The first thing that will come into your mind is going to be fear, which in most people renders them immobile for a few moments. It gives us time for our brain to catch up with our body and provide the best reaction. For someone who has never seen a bear or gone through Girl Scouts, Boy Scouts or other training—the instinct is to run. However, for those who have been through training, it is easier to remain immobile, assess and determine how to make the most noise and appear larger than one is.

A lot can go through your mind in any situation. A person who survived when a bear broke in was not alone. This person had someone else who was already going for a weapon and was trying to keep the dog from attacking the black bear.

The first thing that went through her mind when she heard, "There is a bear in the house," was—what? The words did not penetrate. When the statement was repeated, her brain was able to understand because the bear appeared eight feet from her, coming up from a lower level and raising its head over a railing.

The next reaction was, "Yes, you're right. There is a bear. What should I do?" The other person made noise, so she could edge back down the hallway and get to an exit door, which she opened, she debated opening the screen door too, and then per instructions given to her, locked herself safely in a different area, so the larger person could make noise and help the bear find the exit. Thankfully, this person met a black bear, which is known to be less fearsome and aggressive. The bear was also extremely frightened and just wanted to find a way out. It did not attempt to stand up or growl but rather ran away from the noise in the hope of getting back out any door or window available.

Think about what you might have done in this situation—would you have been able to remain calm or would you have tried to run?

This same individual also had a car catch fire. She managed to avoid stopping at a gas station and rolled into an empty area of a parking lot. In her haste to get to the retail store for help, she took her keys but left her purse. Her thought that no one would approach the burning car to steal the purse and to take the keys was automatic when parking a car. Inside, she waited until the customer service representative was not with a client and then she said, "I think my car is on fire." She didn't panic or break proper manners to interrupt everyone to have the fire department called quicker.

Sometimes what is ingrained in us from an early age, such as proper manners, is hard to get over in any situation. Again, what would you do in that situation? Would you have run in, say "Excuse me, my car is on fire call 911 now please!" or run in screaming "Fire"? Until something happens to you, it is hard to gauge how you would react, but training ensures you have skills to fall back on, even if you panic at first.

Equipment

You need a first aid kit that has everything for superficial wounds, deep wounds, broken bones, burns and the typical malady. If you live in an area with known viruses, you may want to have some natural remedies that can help. For example, a person residing in a rattlesnake environment will have over-the-counter treatments for snake venom, if not the antidote. Purchasing snake bite kits is possible.

You also want emergency road kits based on your areas, such as a blizzard road kit that comes with warming packs and specialized blankets. You can purchase oxygen bottles too, which can help in various situations from dive accidents to altitude sickness.

You always want to have a fire extinguisher in your vehicle in the event your car catches fire, nearby lightning sparks a fire, or if someone is lighting a campfire and causes an incident.

Once you take specialized training courses, you can buy other equipment based on the disasters in your area. Furthermore, you should familiarize yourself with potential emergency equipment on planes since you are no longer able to take most emergency items in a carry-on. You may also consider packing a bag to check that will have allowable emergency items in it.

The more you prepare, the better.

Chapter 2: Natural Disasters

Surviving a natural disaster is possible, but it takes preparedness. You know what types of natural disasters are likely to occur in the area you live. If you go on vacation, you will need to determine the natural disasters that could affect you in your holiday spot.

For example, if you live in Colorado, then blizzards, avalanches, wildfires, flooding, and high wind can lead to trouble. For those who live in Texas, along with the Gulf Coast, and up the Atlantic Coast then hurricanes are the primary concern. Mexico and the western states are often plagued with earthquakes. Midwestern states are known for their tornadoes.

Some storms are predictable. We are aware that they are coming, such as hurricanes and snow storms. However, no one knows when a wildfire might start due to a lightning storm. No one can predict when a tornado will occur, although there is a season when they are more likely. It is difficult to say an earthquake is coming, except when scientists see an increase in tectonic plate movement.

If you live in other parts of the world, sandstorms, typhoons, and other natural disasters can occur. Some are predictable, and others are not, so you always need to have a plan in place to know what you will do if something happens.

The Plan

1. Store food that you can eat for a month. Canned goods and boxed goods are the best choices because they can last a long time and be on hand when you need them.

2. Store enough water for a month. If you do not have a well, then buy gallons of water. For your emergency preparation, you can buy five-gallon jugs and a little stand to use should you need it. For drinking, the rule is eight glasses of water per day, at 8 ounces, which is a half gallon per person. You can survive on less, but if you have the storage make sure you have a half-gallon per person.

3. You will also need water for other things, such as cooking, bathing and wound care. In a time when water is at a premium, you want to have fewer food items that require food and only bathe the critical areas of the body versus taking an entire shower. If you have water, you can also continue to use your toilet, although, for the short term, it is not going to harm the environment if you need to dig a hole for bodily waste.

4. Power is an issue if you live in a cold environment. If you can afford a generator, get one, and have it linked to your power. Also if possible, install solar or wind

energy to help during times of power loss. You can design off-grid power systems that help you keep warm. They are expensive, so it may not be something you can do right away, but you should save up for it.

5. Stock propane for your grill or small camping stoves. Again, you want to have enough to cook at least one meal a day for a month.

With most natural disasters power should be restored within a few weeks, but it may not happen if millions are affected. It is best to have preparations in place that will get you through a month without the necessities.

6. Have an evacuation route or three. Some places like the Keys only have one direction to go, until you hit the central area of Florida. However, you should still have a plan and decide the best time and way to leave. For example, if you know three days ahead of time that a hurricane or snow storm is coming your way, then you can decide if you want to leave your home until it is over. Most of us cannot afford such things unless there is a mandatory evacuation, but this is where saving up comes in. You can also purchase insurance policies that help cover costs if something occurs.

Drive the evacuation routes. You want to be sure you know the roads. Panic will always set in for people who are not as prepared. However, if you think through what is possible, it makes it easier to face what happens.

Another way to get through any disaster is to find the fun in everything. Make it a game to get your preparations completed, as well as during the incident. It may sound odd to say it, let alone think it, but if you can find a little joy—smiling will help you get through even if you are tired, hurt or someone you care about is injured.

The Kit

Everyone knows that an emergency kit with first aid supplies
is necessary. There are several you can buy, and if you look at
survival kits for your area, you get the correct supplies.
Cabela's and other sporting stores also have plenty of
survival/emergency kits.

You can buy defibrillators now to help restart a person's heart.
You can also purchase oxygen bottles. There are a lot of things
you can buy and find in a natural disaster. You need to know
how to use them.

What you may not find in any kit, is ways to contact help. Yes,
you have cell phones, but what if those towers are down? How
can you get emergency services to you when someone is hurt?
In your kit, you will want a few items that will alert services.
For example, Hum is Verizon's answer to emergency and
driving records. You can use Hum to track how you drive or if
there are things wrong with your vehicle. You can also use it to
call 911. So, your vehicle should have some alert system.

Satellite phones are expensive, but if you can afford one, they
are great to have. CBs still work. Police use them, and you can
use the emergency channel to get help. A landline is also not
bad to have if you live in an area where natural disasters occur

regularly. If power is out, the landline will not work, but at least in most situations, it will.

Above all, listen to the news, read the weather online, and determine if you need to enact your emergency plans to avoid becoming a statistic. If you can leave your area before something happens, then do so. Do not hesitate. Those who stay behind thinking they will not come to harm are usually the ones that die.

Chapter 3: War

War is different to a natural disaster. Nature kills indiscriminately, and you often do not have a choice in when such a thing will happen. With war, the signs that something is coming your way exist. However, it does not mean you can get out of the way before things go from bad to worse.

Most of us have never thought about the war coming to our country and affecting us, yet, Europe is plagued with issues due to Isis, which are creating terror attacks and civil unrest in countries like France, England and Germany.

It would be silly not to think about what might happen if some of the threats become a reality. North Korea is still conducting missile tests despite the sanctions and answering tests by Japan, the US, and South Korea. Guam was named as the first target of North Korea. In a statement, the leader said the missile could reach the US, and independent scientists have confirmed this.

It is best not to assume you are safe, simply because you live in a country that has not physically seen the war in a hundred plus years. You may also decide that joining the military if another attack happens is the way to help your family and country.

Knowing how to survive in war is important, even if you think it will not directly affect you as it may others. The fact is there are different types of battles, some are just more like civil unrest, like gang wars versus all-out wars in the Middle East is always seeing.

All of the preparations for natural disasters still apply. Stocking up, being ready to leave with a go bag, and ensuring you have food and water to survive on are necessary even in war.

The difference is some things you may be able to take with you, what you need to leave behind, and whether you can move safely from your home.

Many people decide a bunker is the best way to go. They put their survival gear inside, run power to it for the short term, and hope to survive if bombs, fires, and other war issues arise. Some try to leave with only what they can carry.

Survival is based on how close you are to the attacks. Your best option is to go directly to your embassy or consulate when the fighting gets closer to your home. Take only what you can put in a vehicle or walk with, so you can move fast. Depending on the scale of the war, you may not be able to leave your country and find a haven.

If leaving is not an option, then preparing for the worst attacks, including bullet wounds, and the like, you will want to have as much triage supplies as you can, along with hidden food stores.

Surviving off-grid is another way you may decide to live when war edges closer to you. If you raise your chickens, fruits, vegetables, and other food, then you may be able to survive for years without stepping foot into a city or any food market.

Big targets in war are usually populated areas because it is easier to take out enemies or cause a disruption in these regions. Small farms hidden from view or main paths can sometimes be safer, but not always.

To survive in war, you must be willing to come to your self-defense. If you can, have at least one firearm on the premises that everyone in your family knows how to use. Make it a weapon that you can aim and hit the target, as well as one that provides maximum damage.

Take firearms courses to become more proficient with your aim and more comfortable with the gun.

Additionally, prepare now with a close combat training course. Martial arts and other close combat training help you figure out how to get out of holds if someone gets close to you.

You can also learn how to hold a knife and use it against another person.

Training in this manner will save you. You still have to overcome your fear and hope a bullet does not stop you before you are aware of the threat; however, the more you train for different situations, the better off you are going to be. You will be able to fight your panic and fear, to take action, instead of allowing someone to walk up to you and kill you.

Lastly, if you know you cannot leave your country, you know insurgents are coming, then you may want to leave everything behind and get to a location with family or friends that are in less troubled areas. If not, hunker down, prepare, and do your best to fight for what is yours.

Chapter 4: Civil Unrest

Civil unrest happens in every country. For example, in the US, the south is usually plagued with civil unrest relating to racial issues. The increase in crackdowns for illegal immigrants from Mexico and other Spanish countries south of the border has grown the unrest in certain states. Civil wars continue to break out in the Middle East.

How can you survive if you find yourself in the midst of a storm?

1. Research an area before you travel there, even if it is in your home state.

2. Civil unrest can break out without warning. However, there are usually events that led up to it.

3. Watch the news, determine if there are things that are affecting an area you wish to travel to.

4. Know the routes out of a city or town should an issue arise.

5. Have access to GPS on your phone, map programs, and highlight routes out of the area you are traveling too on a regular map.

6. Have a go-bag with you at all times. This bag should have a day of water, a bit of food, clothing, and an emergency kit.

7. Know where the police station is. How many routes can you take to the nearest police station?

8. Mark the hospitals on your map. How close is the closest one and how many routes can you take to get there?

9. Where is your embassy or consulate if you are in a major city? Again how can you get there?

10. Be prepared to make noise with a whistle, yelling, or anything else. Noise often scares the aggressor, unless there is already a lot of noise. If you cannot yell or scream to bring attention to the attacker, then find a building you can enter, lock the door, and hunker down until you know it is safe.

You may not be in a place with buildings. Civil unrest can happen out in a desert too. You have to create a plan based on the area you are going to be in or where you live.

For example, if someone left their mountain town to visit a large city like Denver, they would want to know which areas are safest to visit and which areas have high crime. Denver's downtown has become something of an unsafe situation.

Unless necessary, most residents stay away from downtown, unless they are in big groups or going to see a performance. They also know where the police are likely to be and the various ways back to their parked car should something occur like a gang war.

The key to survival in an area of civil unrest is to put distance between you and the fighting. Whether you can enter a building, hide behind bushes and trees, or dig a hole in the sand to make it appear as if you do not exist is helpful. You do not want the aggressors to spot you because they will go with their adrenaline and react.

You may have a home in an area of civil unrest. If this is the case, lock the doors, put the shutters down or curtains across the windows, and keep the lights off. Yes, someone might break in if they think it is empty, but the chances are low. Most of the time adrenaline is pumping, and moving targets are the first to be affected.

If you can plan now to set up a bunker or area of your home that is difficult to find. For example, if you have a basement or attic, put supplies in those areas and get inside if unrest comes to your neighborhood.

Chapter 5: Terror Attacks

Terror attacks are even harder to plan for than natural disasters, civil unrest, and war. Typically, there are inklings that issues will occur, such as heightened tensions between two warring factions that lead to knowledge that civil unrest or war will break out. With terror attacks, yes there are media reports. Threats do occur, but as the US saw with 9-11-01, it does not matter what you know in the government or what the papers report, an action can take place that no one thought would occur.

London has recently seen several terror attacks without the police being able to stop them. Terror attacks lead to a high death toll, and you may be one of them simply because you are not aware of any potential threat.

1. Always be aware of your surroundings.

2. Observe the people around you.

3. Put your phone away and pay attention to where you are walking and who is around you.

4. Be vigilante even in mundane locations. Airports, bus terminals, ferry terminals, and other public areas may have a higher terrorist threat level, but walking along

the street can also lead to your involvement in a terrorist attack.

5. Public locations during holidays are more likely targets than your average day.

6. Report anything that is suspicious, such as a left bag, a car that circles the block, etc. It is better to make a report than to leave yourself open to danger because of inaction.

7. If you are in an area of trouble, and something happens, you should always have your emergency kit nearby or on you. You can save yourself, your family, and others around you.

8. Know the routes out of the city.

9. Figure out the different ways back to your vehicle.

10. Learn where emergency services are, including the hospitals, police stations, and other first response teams.

The way to survive when there is a terror attack is first to be vigilant. Most people around them forget that in public dangers do exist. Working in an airport, they have color levels for when threats are higher. A worker has to know what those levels mean to determine if more threats could happen or if there is little activity to worry about. Workers still need to watch, assess, and take note of any strange behavior.

You can adopt these same practices where you work, live, or visit. You can always observe what is going on around you, listen for possible threats, and be ready to dial 911 or whatever emergency number your country uses. The point is, if you are aware of your surroundings, even while entertaining yourself with a book, tablet, or another device, then you can react quicker to attack.

You may not be able to stop what occurs, but you will be able to try and save yourself and those around you before something happens. It is when we fail to think about what may happen that we usually end up in trouble or worse dead.

You cannot control other people, but if you are aware of your surroundings, the chances are making it out because you do not panic are better than if you think life is always going to be okay for you and your family.

In any public location, make sure you know where the exits are, how close you are to them, and if you need to go a different way because the exits may become blocked. If you survive the initial terror attack, fire, gunshots, and panic can be the cause of death.

Surviving an Attack

1. Let the panic in.

2. Use your fear to react versus remain still.

3. To turn your fear into a useful entity, you will need to
    train. Training involves thinking of the scenarios that
    can occur. You do not want to be a doomsday thinker all
    the time, but you should at least assess different
    situations.

What would you do on an airplane if it you are a hostage? Do
you know where the exits are? How do you use the flotation
device, the air, or prepare for a hard landing? What if someone
is standing ten feet away with an explosive device? How would
you save yourself and others?

A lot of surviving an attack is thinking through what you might
do in a situation. It may not help if you become involved in a
situation, but you are teaching your brain how to think in
panic. You are teaching your mind how to assess even when
there is fear.

Often when fear exists we do not know how we will react, but
the more prepared we are for situations, the easier it is for our

mind to come up with some plan, even if it is not the one you original thought about.

Plan, decide on an action and follow through with the situation at hand.

Conclusion

You will survive. Whether you face a natural disaster, war, civil unrest, or terror attack, you have the skills to think through the problem, use your fear for good, and help others. Your preparation, no matter what occurs, will contribute to saving you and others.

You can take control of your family's safety, instead of quaking in fear with them. It will take a little while to gather all the supplies and equipment you need if you have not started already. If you lack any of the tools, supplies and equipment mentioned make sure you get them as soon as you can.

And finally, if you liked the book, I would like to ask you to do me a favor and leave a review for the book on Amazon.